A souvenir guide

Coleton Fishacre
Devon

National Trust

The Art of Country Living

In the 1920s Rupert and Lady Dorothy D'Oyly Carte were sailing along the south Devon coast. Looking for a country retreat, they were inspired to make this beautiful valley running down to the sea the site for an elegant home where they could entertain in style and indulge their passion for the outdoors.

Coleton Fishacre's glorious coastal setting is what first drew the seafaring D'Oyly Cartes here

Careful owners

The D'Oyly Carte family lived at Coleton Fishacre until 1949, when Rupert's daughter Bridget sold it to Rowland Smith, a well-known London motor trader and owner of the Palace Hotel in Torquay. For over 30 years the house and garden were maintained with care until the death of Rowland's wife, Freda, in 1982. The property was then sold to the National Trust.

Preparing for the public

That same year the National Trust opened the garden to visitors, whilst the house was tenanted. Very little in the way of furnishings survived from the time of the D'Oyly Cartes and, with the end of the tenancy in 1997, the National Trust began to prepare the house for public opening. Coleton Fishacre was first fully presented to visitors in 1999, with much of the house open to view. Since that time the collection has been enhanced by the National Trust to reflect the house's heyday in the 1930s. The whole house, with the exception of a few rooms for offices, kitchen and rest room, is now open for visitors to enjoy.

Rupert was the son of Richard D'Oyly Carte, the impresario behind the hugely popular operettas of Gilbert and Sullivan. He developed the business empire he inherited, including the Savoy Hotel and Claridge's in London. Such outlets for luxury and entertainment during the post-War period, set against a backdrop of political unrest, marches and strikes, responded to patrons' needs with huge success.

Arts and Crafts

Building for Coleton Fishacre began in 1923 to the design of Oswald Milne (1881–1967), an architect who had worked as an assistant to Edwin Lutyens from 1902 to 1905. Inspired by the influence of the Arts and Crafts Movement and its beliefs in simple design and high standards of craftsmanship, the house responded to its landscape and literally grew out of it. The stone came from a quarry in the garden and the design embraced the beauty of the surroundings.

Above Enjoying the view out to sea from the Gazebo

Above The house photographed from the Gazebo in 1930

The D'Oyly Cartes

Left Richard D'Oyly Carte

Bottom left *The Gondoliers* (1889) was the climax of Gilbert and Sullivan's decade of success at the Savoy Theatre

Richard D'Oyly Carte (1844–1901) started his career in his father's music publishing and musical instrument business. He went on to build two of London's theatres and a hotel empire, while also establishing an opera company that ran continuously for over a hundred years and a management agency representing some of the most important artists of the day.

Born into a musical family, Richard composed operas as a young man, moving on to work as a concert agent and theatrical manager in 1870.

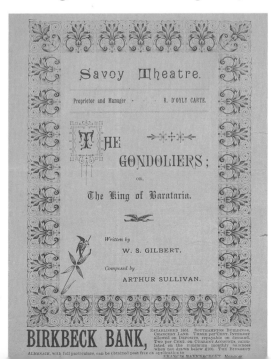

In 1875, *Trial by Jury* was the first operetta to combine the forces of wordsmith and barrister W.S. Gilbert with those of the talented young composer Arthur Sullivan. Richard had discovered a unique combination. These operettas' memorable tunes, ingenious and gently satirical plot lines and moral acceptability to the middle classes saw a string of hugely successful shows and the establishment of the Savoy Theatre off the Strand.

Opera's populist

A string of hit shows followed, from *HMS Pinafore* in 1878, through *The Pirates of Penzance* (1879), *Iolanthe* (1882), *The Mikado* (1885), *The Yeomen of the Guard* (1888) to *The Gondoliers* in 1889. These formed the basis of the D'Oyly Carte Opera Company's permanent repertoire, performed both at the Savoy Theatre and by touring companies across Britain and the United States. Their premières at the Savoy every year or two were major social events, with Sullivan himself conducting the orchestra. The annual profits for the company reached £60,000 and songs from the operettas were heard and sung in homes all over the world.

Rupert the moderniser

On Richard's death in 1901, the family business was managed by his second wife, Helen Couper-Black and then passed to his son Rupert, first as Chairman of the Savoy Hotel Company in 1903 and then manager of the opera company in 1913.

Little had been done since 1900 to reflect changes in style, with the wardrobe mistress still issuing the female chorus with red flannel knickers, and Rupert approached the challenges of modernising the businesses with energy and a discerning eye. His patronage of artists and designers of the period resulted in such innovations as new sets and costumes for *The Mikado*, commissioned from the distinguished artist Charles Ricketts and accurately based on Japanese fashions of around 1720; they were praised as 'almost embarrassing in their wealth'.

He also introduced to his hotels new interiors in a refined French Art Deco style. The Savoy Theatre, rebuilt by Rupert in 1929 to the designs of Frank Tugwell, saw astonishing new interiors of shimmering silver-leaf and designs in red, orange and yellow, inspired by zinnias in Hyde Park.

Separated in grief

Rupert and Lady Dorothy had two children, Bridget, born in 1908, and Michael born in 1911. The tragic death of their son aged just 21 in a car accident in Switzerland (see page 18) was a huge blow, undermining their marriage and resulting in their separation in 1936. On Rupert's death in 1948, Coleton Fishacre was sold by Bridget, who lived in London, and the family's ownership of the property came to an end.

Above The programme for *The Mikado* at the Savoy Theatre

Top The entrance of the Savoy Theatre by night

Left Rupert D'Oyly Carte

The building of Coleton Fishacre

Having found their plot of land, Rupert and Lady Dorothy D'Oyly Carte set about the task of finding an architect who could make their vision a reality. They wanted a modern home but in a rustic style. Quarried from local stone, the house they built sits very naturally in its spectacular coastal setting.

Their architect was Oswald Milne, one-time protégé of Sir Edwin Lutyens, but by the time he came to draw plans for the D'Oyly Cartes, he was an established architect in his own right. His building at Coleton Fishacre is now regarded as his finest work and one of the most successful country houses to be built in the 1920s.

The plan of Coleton Fishacre forms three unequal arms of a Y, with the entrance courtyard to the north-east, a service entrance against the slope of the hill to the north and the garden stretching to the south. Although not a new design, Milne's skill was in embracing and maximising the surroundings, allowing the house to be at one with its landscape.

Rupert and Lady Dorothy, keen to keep a close eye on the construction work of the contractors E.H. Burgess of Berners Street, London, rented a house in nearby Kingswear. The groundwork was begun in January 1925 and the house completed in June of the following year.

Left Coleton Fishacre was robustly constructed from local stone to take full advantage of the views from its spectacular setting

Right (above) The granite paving, laid in a radiating pattern, is a striking feature of the forecourt

Right (below) The material, quarried from the garden itself, was used in constructing both the house and its garden terraces and walls

Material matters

Enhanced by the fine quality of the Delabole slates and their curving designs, encompassing both the semi-circular bay on the garden front and roof ridge of the service quarters sliding forward over the Loggia (see page 23), the roofline is key to the design, giving the house a flow and sense of unity. Dartmouth shale stone for the walls, with its subtle mixture of blues, greens and browns, set off by thick mortar joints, continues into the garden terracing and walls. The leaded casement windows, surrounded by unpainted oak sub frames, and the restrained use of any decorative features to its exterior, all serve to enhance the quality of craftsmanship and beauty of materials.

This quality extends to the radiating granite paving in the forecourt, the stone-walling of the garden and even to the outbuildings: a 'motor lodge' to house the D'Oyly Carte's Bentley, a chauffeur's flat and two staff cottages, which, although less expensively built out of brick and rendered, nevertheless followed the same principles of quality and design.

Local transport

The building material was blasted from rock in the lower part of the combe (where the Gazebo [see page 46] stands today) and transported to the site by a small temporary railway. Rupert D'Oyly Carte kept a photographic record of Coleton Fishacre beginning in 1924 and finishing in November 1937; taken in May 1925 this shows the railway track that transported the quarried stone.

Life at Coleton Fishacre

Coleton Fishacre provided the perfect setting for the outdoor life the D'Oyly Cartes so enjoyed. Lady Dorothy spent a lot of time here, whilst Rupert came down from their London home at 6 Derby Street every Friday evening for the weekend.

The garden, developed from a valley of hedged pastures and orchards, flourished under their enthusiasm. The couple's many sailing trips included moorings so that they could visit gardens in south Cornwall, seeking out inspiration. On Saturday mornings they would walk around their garden discussing plans for future planting, which Rupert would detail in his plant lists and which were then realised by Lady Dorothy and her gardener, Jack Sharland.

'The place belongs to the sea ... here is a retreat from land-sickness, a spot where hurries and worries and work do not come.'

Christopher Hussey,
Country Life, 1930

Outdoor entertainment

Entertaining formed an important part of life at Coleton Fishacre. Amongst the many weekend guests were musicians, such as the conductor Sir Malcolm Sargent, and the painter Charles Ricketts. These visitors would take part in bridge parties and various outdoor pursuits. In addition to sailing, Rupert was a very keen fisherman, illustrated by the weathervane on the roof, and had a passion for shooting.

One of their favourite pastimes was spending time in Pudcombe Cove (see page 44), a private beach at the bottom of the garden. There the family would soak up the sun and swim, either in the sea or in the tidal seawater bathing pool which they created. Every comfort was catered for, from a changing hut to a cold-water shower, made by diverting a stream. At the end of the day, on the ringing of the ship bell above the Bowling Green Lawn near the house, the family would return for pre-dinner drinks.

Above The house at Coleton Fishacre exists for its views of the sea

The end of an era

This idyllic lifestyle was, sadly, not to last. In 1932 the death of their son (see page 18) put huge pressure on their marriage and they separated in 1936. Rupert continued to live at Coleton Fishacre and, in 1939, welcomed Brigadier General and Kitty Llewellyn, whose home in Nethway House had been requisitioned for evacuees from a school in Plymouth. They remained at Coleton Fishacre until Rupert's death in 1948.

Bridget D'Oyly Carte had, during this time, been deeply involved with the family's businesses and with child welfare work in London. In 1926 she had married her cousin, later the 4th Earl of Cranbrook, but the marriage only lasted for four years. In 1948 Bridget took over the running of the opera company from her father and formed the D'Oyly Carte Opera Trust, a charity devoted to the promotion of future productions.

Top By June 1935, when this photo was taken, the house was settling into the softening landscape of the D'Oyly Cartes' garden

Middle Brigadier General Llewellyn admiring the view

Right Ringing the bell for pre-dinner drinks

Later owners

The D'Oyly Cartes created a wonderful weekend retreat here, stylish and comfortable with views of the sea that would never grow old and a garden that would continuously delight. But, inevitably, the time came when the care and enjoyment of Coleton Fishacre passed to new owners.

Bridget sold Coleton Fishacre in 1949 to Rowland Smith and his wife Freda. Rowland, whose father George owned a garage in Camden Town, had been a despatch rider for the RNAS in the First World War and opened his own motor showroom in London in the early 1920s. The business developed into Rowland Smith Motors Ltd and became one of the largest and best known in the trade. Business boomed and, on 1 January 1961, Rowland bought himself a Rolls Royce Silver Cloud II, with the Registration Number RSM 1, in which he travelled from Devon to London a few times a year. Whilst his car was garaged and treasured, Freda's Mk VII Jaguar was used daily.

Rowland's business closed down in the late 1960s and he and Freda became the owners of the Palace Hotel in Torquay which, after suffering major damage during the Second World War, had been restored and re-opened in 1948.

The garden on show

The Smiths lived at, and cared for, Coleton Fishacre for over 30 years. Rowland died in 1979 and the estate was offered for sale to the National Trust by Freda, just before her death in January 1982. The National Trust initially acquired the estate in order to link up land it owned on the south Devon coast path. However, the outstanding quality of the garden soon became apparent and it was opened to the public almost immediately.

The house, meanwhile, was let to private tenants. Little in the way of contents had been left behind from the D'Oyly Cartes' time, the exceptions being the Dining Room furniture and the Marion Dorn carpets, and the tenants furnished the house themselves, for a while offering bed and breakfast to the public.

Dressing the house

In 1998, at the end of the tenancy, the National Trust opened parts of Coleton Fishacre once a month with limited contents. After much research and the acquisition of suitable furnishings, the house fully opened to visitors for the first time in 1999. The 1930 *Country Life* article on the house by Christopher Hussey and a 1949 inventory of contents proved to be invaluable sources of reference.

From top
Rowland Smith and his wife Freda in the garden

Rowland and Freda Smith outside the Loggia

The Smiths continued to enjoy and maintain the D'Oyly Cartes' garden

Right The 1949 inventory of contents

STUDY.

A low fender-seat, upholstered in brown leather, fitted to fireplace.   12. -. -.

LIBRARY.

A painting show... ...ndscape and
Seascape of "... ..." and
environments
frame; 6'6"
Vane in circ...
This fits i...

A light polis...
the shaped
stered in

A polished
with glaz...

LOUNGE.

Four pairs of beige figured brocatelle curtains to cill length, the valances, and a pair of ditto to casement doors, with valance (all worn).

A cream hand made wool carpet 20' x 15'.   40. -.

225. -.
12. -.
10. -.

...arpeting

...g edge,
...pp, and
...lvet loose   45. -.

...uction
..., cane
...ream linen.   65. -.

...with
... x 2'6"   36. -.

...   30. -.

...tool   2. 15. -.

...wood
...into
... etc.
... wide.   18. -. -.

...high
...tered
...ved

... table   10. -. -.
... top.   3. 10. -.

ITEMS DELETED FROM THE INVENTORY OF THE TENANT'S FITTINGS AT THE

COLETON ESTATE, BRIXHAM.

POTTING SHED.

9 garden forks, 2 long handle manure forks.

4 garden spades.

4 Dutch hoes.

3 pick axes.

3 long handle shovels.

3 mattocks.

3 garden rakes.

1 turnip hoe.

1 cross cut saw, 5 ft.

1 ditto, 3'6".

Art Deco in Devon

In contrast to the late 19th-century Arts and Crafts style of the exterior, the interior of Coleton Fishacre is dramatically 20th-century Art Deco in design.

Simplicity, quality and finish are key to the interiors of the house. The rooms, and the corridors in particular, are almost austere in their lack of ornament. Walls run into ceilings with a smooth continuous curve, and furnishings – a mixture of baroque and oriental – are tastefully spaced out in pale rooms with accents of strong colour typical of the 1920s.

Below (left) The first-floor corridor photographed by *Country Life* in 1930 shows the minimalist style to which the D'Oyly Cartes aspired

Below (right) The main staircase in the same year, four years after building finished

Staircase
Information Room and Yellow Bathroom

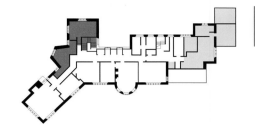

The main staircase, with its great sweep of panelled pale limed oak and varnished top rail, is testimony to the beauty of materials and quality of craftsmanship. The honeycomb ceiling lights, original to the house, relieve the austerity of the scheme.

Above the landing hangs a large painting by Walter Richard Sickert (1860–1942) of St Mark's, Venice, described in 1930 by Christopher Hussey in *Country Life* as providing a 'splash of mellow colour on the whitewashed walls'. Placed there by the D'Oyly Cartes, it was later given by Dame Bridget to the British Council in appreciation for all the amateur Gilbert and Sullivan productions it had supported around the world and hangs here once again thanks to a generous loan by its owner.

Turn right into the Information Room.

Once Bridget's bedroom, this room is now used to give background information on the D'Oyly Cartes, the building of Coleton Fishacre, the architectural styles of the day and the house's later occupants. A display cabinet houses Gilbert and Sullivan memorabilia and the model of the house was created from original drawings by Oswald Milne.

Turn right along the Bedroom Corridor.

The Bedroom Corridor, carpeted by the previous tenants in 1991–92 and with simpler versions of the honeycomb ceiling light fittings, runs the entire length of the house. On your right is the bathroom that served the main bedroom; a panel has been designed to give an idea of the space behind it, since it was later modernised and no longer retains its original features.

Follow the corridor to the end.

Below The honeycomb ceiling lights are original to the house

Lady Dorothy's Bedroom

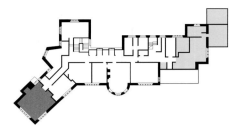

This room, one of the largest of the seven bedrooms, was used by Rupert and Lady Dorothy when the house was built in 1926. We have been able to recreate the layout of the room very accurately, thanks to the photographic evidence in the 1930 *Country Life* article.

The original fireplace had been removed but a replica travertine marble copy was reinstated in 2006. Only two pieces of furniture remain from the D'Oyly Cartes' time: the upholstered dressing table stool and the cupboard to the right of the fireplace, the remaining pieces being reproduced in 2005 by a company from Looe.

The reproduction of the *Les Arums* design by Raoul Dufy on the curtains and cushions is a particular triumph of research. This involved the identification of the pattern, the discovery of the original printing blocks in the archives of the Lyons textile firm Bianchini Ferier in France and the final printing of the design onto cream linen by the same firm. The near-black carpet was made by Axminster Carpets to reproduce the original. The portrait of a lady in a large hat by Raymond, originally purchased by Richard D'Oyly Carte, is now displayed thanks to the generosity of the owner.

The room has extensive views across the grounds, over the Rill Garden, which was originally planted with roses so beloved by Lady Dorothy, and down the valley towards the sea.

Retrace your steps down the Bedroom Corridor and turn right into Rupert's Dressing Room.

Additional guests
The bat screen in the central window is evidence of the use of the house by bats and the interdependence of house, garden and estate.

Left Lady Dorothy was the third and youngest daughter of the 2nd Earl of Cranbrook

Right Lady Dorothy's dressing table; the stool is one of the few pieces of furniture original to the house

Rupert's Dressing Room

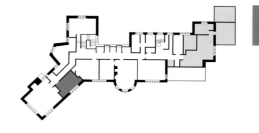

This room would have served as a dressing room to the neighbouring bedroom, probably used in the main by Rupert. In contrast to Lady Dorothy's Bedroom, there was no evidence on which to base the furnishing for this room and so we have created a room based on research of such rooms at that period.

The broad mullioned windows have black Staffordshire tile sills, like all the windows in the house, and beautiful attention to detail in the design of the ironwork fittings.

Dressing rooms are a particularly English refinement, first appearing in the second half of the 17th century to signify a room for the reception of the closest of visitors or guests. By the early 19th century such rooms were restricted to the storage of clothes and for dressing, sometimes also offering a sense of retreat and privacy.

Return to the Bedroom Corridor and turn right.

Domestic design
The three linen cupboards on the left along the bedroom corridor, each with double limed oak doors, are heated by the hot water pipes that feed the radiators here.

Right The quality of construction can be clearly seen in the windows

Guest accommodation

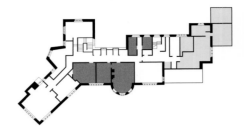

The three rooms on the seaward side of the Bedroom Corridor – the Guest Bedroom, Turret Dressing Room and Turret Bedroom – and their accompanying bathrooms on the opposite side comprised the guest accommodation at Coleton Fishacre.

With the D'Oyly Cartes' love of entertaining and inviting weekend guests, this suite of rooms would have been much used, particularly in the summer months.

No original furniture remains for these rooms, nor is there any evidence of how they looked, with the exception of the main furniture which was described in the 1949 inventory. They have been furnished by the National Trust with Heal's oak bedroom furniture to evoke the 1930s. The 'Bestlite' anglepoise lamp, however, is original to the Dressing Room and dates from the 1920s or 1930s.

With the departure of Lady Dorothy, following the break-up of her marriage to Rupert, and the arrival of Brigadier General Llewellyn and his wife Kitty in 1939 (see page 9), this suite of rooms continued to be used by houseguests.

Separate quarters

Among the houseguests that used the comfortable but segregated accommodation at Coleton Fishacre were the Llewellyns' son, Major George Llewellyn, and his girlfriend, Loveday Bolitho. George slept in the Turret Bedroom and recalls the furore caused when Loveday was found sitting on his bed, comforting him when he was ill. The episode did not prevent the couple later marrying.

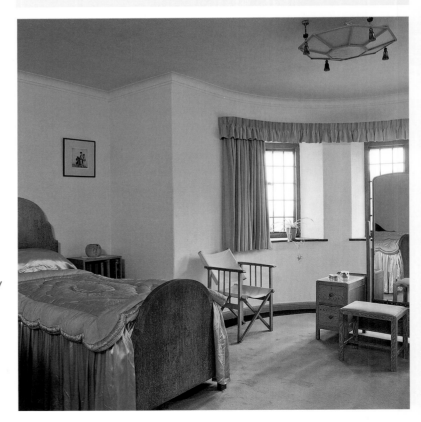

Right **The Turret Bedroom**

Opposite Edward Bawden tiles over the towel rail in the male guests' bathroom (The Estate of Edward Bawden)

His and hers bathrooms

Opposite the bedrooms are the bathrooms, for male and female guests respectively. They retain many of their original fittings including the Doulton & Co. sunken baths. The green glass soap dishes and blue glass sponge bowls were recreated especially for the house by Dartington Glass, as the originals were in pieces.

The plain tiles of the walls are interspersed with pictorial tiles designed by Edward Bawden (1903–90) for Carter's of Poole, who, having recognised his outstanding talents as an illustrator and designer, employed him soon after he graduated from the Royal College of Art. The tiles depict scenes of outdoor life, so appropriate for Coleton Fishacre, and include both traditional sports like fishing and more modern interests such as motorcars.

Right Edward Bawden's tiles appropriately depict sports pursued by country men and women in the two guest bathrooms (The Estate of Edward Bawden)

The East Bedroom

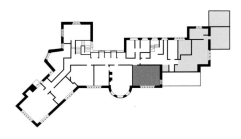

The newspaper reports of the accident, including the *Exeter Express and Echo* on the day itself, 24 October 1932, and *The Times* on the following day, give vivid descriptions of the collision in Switzerland between Michael's MG and a motorcycle, ridden by a young Swiss workman. Michael was in Switzerland on his way to an intensive course of hotel training in Germany, with a view to his taking up a senior position at the Savoy Group. Michael and his passenger, friend Richard Snagge, were both thrown from the car. Michael died instantly, his passenger only slightly hurt. The motorcycle rider died later in hospital. Michael was buried in Switzerland and a plaque can be found in St Mary's Church, Brixham.

Another room with fine views overlooking the garden, the East Bedroom has been furnished by the National Trust with items from the 1920s and 1930s.

Original to the room is the washbasin, with its unusual plug and overflow arrangement. Like all the bedrooms along the corridor the washbasin is backed with remoulded powdered glass tiles. These, made from recycled glass, were also being installed in the refurbished Savoy Hotel in London, owned by the D'Oyly Cartes.

Rupert D'Oyly Carte retired to this end of the house when his marriage to Lady Dorothy was breaking down, following the death of their only son, Michael, aged just 21 (see right). Rupert and Lady Dorothy's marriage never recovered from this and Lady Dorothy left Coleton Fishacre four years later.

Turn right onto the Servants' Landing.

Left All the bedrooms' washbasins and fittings were of the same specification that Rupert D'Oyly Carte was installing in the luxury Savoy Hotel

Servants' quarters

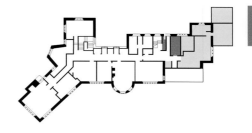

Originally a wing comprising four bedrooms for servants, the National Trust converted these rooms, initially to staff accommodation and later to an office, a kitchen and meeting room for staff and volunteers.

The Maid's Bedroom

During the winter of 2011–12, the National Trust re-created one of the maids' bedrooms and lavatory as it would have looked when the house was built, and opened the rooms to visitors for the first time in 2012. The arrangement of the partition wall between bedrooms at the mid-point of the window was intentional, to make best use of the available light to the two rooms. The corner sink is original to the bedroom and there would have been similar ones in all these rooms. The floors of all the rooms through this part of the house were originally covered with linoleum.

The Sluice Room

The Sluice Room on the right at the top of the Servants' Stairs was essentially a housekeeper's store and is furnished with cleaning equipment from the 1930s. Of particular interest are the Ewbank floor sweeper, the 'Success', costing 36 shillings and 9 pence in 1925 (£1.88), and an early suction cleaner made by Electrolux in its wooden box with attachments. In 1919 the Lux vacuum was the first product Electrolux ever sold. The ceramic sink with attached sluice

sink and hinged metal bucket rest, was made by Royal Doulton and is original to the house. Its use might have included the emptying of chamber pots for visitors.

The cream and brown chequered flooring has been reproduced from the original.

Right A vacuum cleaner and household cleaning equipment in the Sluice Room

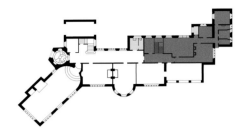

The Butler's Pantry

The Butler's Pantry, close to the Dining Room, was where, amongst other tasks, the butler oversaw the cleaning and safe storage of silver and precious china.

The Belfast sink, with its beech draining board, is original to the house; the glazed storage cupboard, a slightly later introduction. The butler would also have

been responsible for managing the wine cellar, the door and steps to which lead off the Servants' Corridor.

Turn left out of the Butler's Pantry.

The Servants' Corridor

The Servants' Corridor houses the original wall-mounted servants' electric bell system, supplied by T. Clarke & Co. Ltd of 129 Sloane Street, London. This would have been used by the family or their guests to summon servants and is still in working order.

Turn left into the Kitchen.

The Kitchen

The Kitchen was very much the working heart of Coleton Fishacre and would have been a hive of industry, the cook overseeing the preparation and the cooking of meals for the family, their guests and staff.

The screen dividing the room from the corridor is original to the house, found in a barn on the estate, and repaired and reinstated by the National Trust in 2011. The shelf to the left of the sink has also been returned to the room, having been stored in the cellar and identified and reinstated by marrying up holes in the kitchen wall.

The double Belfast sink is supported on sections of the 1925 railway track used to bring stone from the quarry in the garden when building the house (see page 7). This and the plate rack above are original. The dresser is an exact copy of the original Quicksey kitchen cabinet and, thanks to photographic evidence, was made by David Lloyd of Dunkeswell. The paint decoration of the room

Left The electric bell board is the original one and still in working order

was researched in great detail and, using pigment analysis from paint scrapes, the vivid salmon pink was found to be the original scheme.

Pass through the screen and turn left.

The Servants' Hall

The Servants' Hall was the room for staff to eat and relax in their free time. The D'Oyly Cartes were wealthy enough to afford a substantial staff at Coleton Fishacre – butler, housekeeper, housemaid and cook. We have re-created the room to give an idea of how it might have looked, with its dining table, settee and the radiogram made by His Master's Voice. The wall-mounted bookcase is original to the house and listed on the 1949 inventory. The colour of the doors is again based on paint analysis.

Go through the far door and turn right.

Service Rooms

The Drying Room was used to dry clothes which had come from the Laundry at the far end of the passage. The Brushing Room, to its left, was used to brush clothes and to clean shoes, boots and sports equipment. The original soda siphon is a rare survival. A lavatory separates this room from the Laundry, where the original sink and draining board remain.

Retrace your steps along the passage and turn right.

The Larder

The Larder, where food was stored until required, was kept cool by natural ventilation through the original decorated mesh screen in the window. Although there was a refrigerator at Coleton Fishacre, the Larder was still a vital area in domestic management and would have been used to store dry goods as well as fruit and vegetables.

Retrace your steps through the Kitchen screen and turn right and then left.

Left The kitchen sink rests on sections of the railway track used during the construction of the house

Right Art Deco features can even be seen in the Larder

The Dining Room

In contrast to all the other rooms at Coleton Fishacre, the majority of the furniture in the Dining Room is original to the house. This room, with its custom-made furniture and easy access onto the garden, perhaps best exemplifies what the D'Oyly Cartes wanted from their weekend retreat.

Much of the furniture was commissioned by the D'Oyly Cartes from their architect Oswald Milne, including the walnut sideboard, dining table and pair of side tables, which could be moved to extend the main table. The colour of the scagliola table tops, made of plaster of Paris, pigments and animal glue to imitate marble, was chosen to evoke the sea. The lapis lazuli servants' bell push plugs into the floor beneath.

The 1920s chair, upholstered in Florentine flame stitch, is one of the set used by the D'Oyly Cartes and the four opalescent glass Lalique wall lights, of the *Tulipes* design, are also original to the room. The oil painting

above the sideboard, *Boulevard St Germain*, was painted by Bassett Fitzgerald Wilson (1888–1972) in 1930.

The carpet, like that in the rest of the house, was laid by the previous tenants in 1991–92. The 1930 *Country Life* photographs show the original flooring to be a grid-like pattern, but are not clear enough to indicate whether this was linoleum or carpet.

Left **The Dining Room in 1930**

Below **Symmetry and simplicity of design in the Dining Room**

The Loggia

Leading directly from the Dining Room, the Loggia makes an extra 'outdoor' room. Loggias were a very popular feature of houses of this period and this one exploits the setting to its fullest.

With its large table and seating area, the D'Oyly Cartes and their guests would have eaten their meals here during the summertime. The pair of ceiling lights, reproductions of the originals, clearly indicate that it was also used in the evenings. Although protected on three sides by walls and glazing, the Loggia is open on one side to take in views of the garden. The view down the valley is framed by solid slate pillars and softened by the overhanging grapevine and other tender plants.

The Loggia is still a place where visitors can sit and enjoy the views. Indeed, it is a favourite place for the house staff to take their morning coffee on a well-earned break!

Right The Loggia for *al fresco* dining

The Library

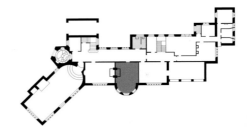

The Library is in the centre of the house, a cosy and intimate room with its bow window to the south. It is fitted with simple pine shelves and lit by simple translucent alabaster uplighters, original to the house.

Dominating the room, above the travertine marble fireplace, is a painted map of the south Devon coast around Coleton Fishacre, which incorporates a wind dial. The painting is by George Spencer Hoffman (1875–1950), an architect-trained artist. Hoffman created a similar map painting for the landlord of the Spread Eagle public house in Thame, a place visited by the D'Oyly Cartes.

The set of four armchairs, although re-covered, are original to the house and the floor is made of Indian gurjan wood, supplied by Howard Bros & Co. Ltd of Commercial Wharf, London. Gathered near the window are a *Vanity Fair* cartoon of Richard D'Oyly Carte by 'Spy' (the *nom de plume* of L.M. Ward) and two 1920s Egyptian watercolours of the River Nile by Chester Silverlock. These, together with the Egyptian sphinxes and clock, make an interesting link with the sundial, visible on the exterior wall of the house through the right-hand window.

Turn left along the corridor.

Personal touches
George Spencer Hoffman's map is a near-realistic bird's-eye view, despite the over-scaled house and also the depiction of Rupert sitting overlooking the combe with his favourite Dalmatian. This was the spot where Rupert's ashes were scattered.

Left The cartoon of Richard by 'Spy'

Right The Library's bookshelves have been restocked but the alabaster uplighters are original

Opposite The Sitting Room

The Sitting Room

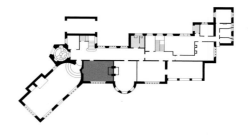

Although much of the furniture in this modestly proportioned room is not original, its scale, together with the light that floods in through the south-facing windows and the views onto the garden give the visitor a good sense of what the D'Oyly Cartes would have enjoyed about this room.

The Sitting Room has another handsome chimneypiece, this time carved from Hopton Wood (in Derbyshire) limestone that is rich in fossils. The pale colour of the walls emphasises the broad mullioned windows with their black Staffordshire tile sills, like all windows in the house. The semi-circular niche opposite the fireplace was designed to display flowers or ceramics and is plastered in a smooth finish in contrast to the rougher walls.

The furniture in this room is not original to the house, although the pair of ebonised bookcases has been reproduced from photographs of the originals. The handsome three-piece suite, with walnut-veneer side panels and velvet upholstery, was designed by Maurice Adams. However, the marble tondo (the circular relief carving to the right of the niche) depicting a boy blowing a conch shell by J. Harvard Thomas, dates from 1893 and was brought to the house by the D'Oyly Cartes.

Turn left along the corridor.

The Saloon

The entrance to the Saloon is intentionally impressive and theatrical, and shows the ingenious way in which Oswald Milne dealt with awkward changes in level of the site, using them to great advantage.

The easy elegance found in the Saloon is of a style that was described and illustrated by Osbert Lancaster as 'Curzon Street Baroque' in his 1939 book *Homes Sweet Homes*. The Saloon offers the comfort demanded by everyday living with a touch of the dramatic. Stage-like, curving steps lead down into a room of generous proportions, almost 12 metres long. The room is set at an angle to the rest of the house to maximise the views down the garden.

Above An illustration of the style 'Curzon Street Baroque'

Right The Saloon in 1930

The fine Siena marble chimneypiece, supplied by Messrs Jenkins & Son of Torquay, is in contrast to the rough plaster finish of the room, subtly accentuated after dark by the Art Deco alabaster wall lights, installed in 1926. There is a pull-down fire screen within the chimney.

The main feature of the room is the windows, overlooking the garden on two sides and with double doors leading out to the terrace to the south. The lack of pictures hanging on the walls was intentional, the windows providing a visual feast of living art.

The floor is laid with Indian gurjan wood and, in the 1930 *Country Life* photograph, was covered with a large French-style carpet spanning the room. Later in the 1930s a new

carpet, runner and pair of rugs were introduced, created for this room by the American Marion Dorn. The runner is a copy of the original, now too worn to use.

The great majority of the furniture has been introduced by the National Trust. The overmantel mirror, its design echoing the details around the door, is a 1999 copy of the original, made by James Bellchambers and Paignton Glassworks. The Bluthner rosewood grand piano, dating from 1895–96, was bought by the National Trust in 2002.

Retrace your steps to the Hall.

Personal touches

Marion Dorn was the leading freelance textile designer of the inter-War period in England. Her style favoured large-scale patterns for her carpets, whose texture of weave was just as important as her simple colour combinations.

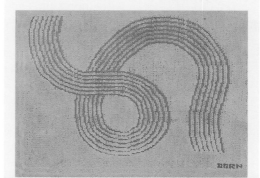

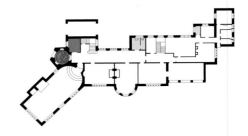

The Flower Room and Porch

At the entrance to the Hall and by the main door to the house are these small but revealing rooms, each with features it would be easy to miss, features that are quietly revealing about life at Coleton Fishacre.

The Flower Room

Opposite is the Flower Room, filled with shelves to store flower vases, and a sink, all original to the house. It was here that cut flowers from the garden were arranged for display in the rooms and this was very much Lady Dorothy's domain. Designing a special room just for this purpose indicates how important cut flowers were to the family, again giving the sensation of bringing the garden indoors. The room was also used as a cloakroom for coats and outdoor clothes. The wall-mounted internal telephone was connected to the garage, located in the Motor Lodge half-way up the drive, and was used to call the chauffeur to bring the car down to the house. The light switch is believed to be original to the house, one of the few surviving.

The Porch

The circular Porch, polygonal on the exterior, has a curved walnut bench, original to the house and initially one of a pair. It was made by Gordon Russell of Broadway in Worcestershire, and would have been accompanied by a curved walnut table, no longer at Coleton Fishacre. The central circular threshold mat, with its Latin inscription *CAVE CANEM* meaning 'beware of the dog', served as a warning to visitors about the family dogs, which included Dalmatians and Cairn Terriers. This one is a copy of the 1920s original, now too worn to be used. Beneath the mat is a central roundel, carved with Rupert and Lady Dorothy's initials and the date the house was completed, 1926.

The front door leads out onto the radiating pattern of granite paving in the forecourt, striking in its simplicity and beauty of execution and large enough to provide a turning circle for the D'Oyly Cartes' Bentley. The use of circular patterns, inspired by Lutyens, is to be found repeated in the garden.

Above The telephone in the Flower Room was connected to the garage

Left The tide-indicator in the Hall was used to indicate high water in Pudcombe Cove and best times for bathing in the tidal pool and sailing

Opposite The initials of Rupert and Lady Dorothy D'Oyly Carte and the date of the completion of the house, 1926, set into the stonework of the Entrance Hall

The Art of Gardening

When the D'Oyly Cartes happened upon this spot, they knew they'd found a special place, but what was here when they arrived was very different to what they left. This exceptional garden in all its many parts is their carefully executed creation.

From open views around the house at the head of the narrow combe and formal terraces, the 24-acre Grade II registered garden at Coleton Fishacre descends through increasingly jungle-like vegetation, following the course of a stream down to the sea at Pudcombe Cove.

The lie of the land

The geology of the area – acidic soil overlying Dartmouth shale and with water running through the valley in many areas – makes this garden suitable for a wide range of plants. One of the botanically richest summer and late-summer gardens cared for by the National Trust, the garden at Coleton Fishacre includes succulents from the Canaries in the upper parts of the garden and tree ferns from New Zealand in the cooler parts of the valley. The atmospheric humidity is high beneath the tree canopy and makes perfect conditions for many moisture-loving plants. This, together with the mild climate, enables species that can survive outside in few other places in Britain to thrive and grow to an exceptional size at Coleton Fishacre.

Every detail planned

Rupert and Lady Dorothy D'Oyly Carte were both enthusiastic gardeners and, keen to ensure the success of their new garden, sought advice from Edward White of the landscape designers Milner & White. Under his guidance, and even before the house had been completed, they planted a woodland shelterbelt of pine, holm oak and sycamore on the bare ridges to provide protection from the strong prevailing winds. With this belt of trees in place, Rupert and Lady Dorothy could then concentrate on planting the garden itself, experimenting with trees and shrubs from around the world. The planting plan took account of future vistas and views, testimony to their far-sighted vision, which is still evident today.

Top Today the house luxuriates in lush, naturalistic planting; but all was devised and designed by the D'Oyly Cartes

Above With the house complete, planting and landscaping could begin in earnest

Opposite The native *Zinnia elegans* is a wild desert plant from Mexico but its garden form does well here

Planning and planting

The book of planting plans kept by Rupert D'Oyly Carte from about 1928 to 1947 noted plants in all 78 beds as they were acquired, together with details of the source and planting location, with additional comments about their performance noted later. Altogether the D'Oyly Cartes planted over 10,000 trees and shrubs.

Plants seem to have been chosen mainly for their aesthetic qualities and suitability for a particular location, rather than any botanical or rarity value. Plants came from 70 different nurseries, chiefly from Hilliers of Winchester, but also from other sources such as holidays in Madeira and Crete. Rupert was meticulous in keeping weather records and his notebooks,

Below (left) Rupert made careful note of what was planted where and how it fared

Below (right) Rupert also recorded daily rainfall

Right Two of the D'Oyly Cartes' gardeners, photographed in May 1929

Below Today three gardeners aided by volunteers keep the garden looking its best

Continuing the work

Today, new challenges face the National Trust. At the garden's height the D'Oyly Cartes had six gardeners, with Mr Jack Sharland as Head Gardener. This number was reduced to one after the Second World War. The Smiths employed five gardeners, later reduced to three, with Head Gardener Mr Eddy Shepperd, who continued to work in the garden when the National Trust acquired it. The National Trust employs three full-time gardeners, supported by a manager and a group of dedicated volunteers. The control of invasive plants and changes in weather patterns, as well as the increase in the number of visitors to the garden, all require the creative management of staff resources.

The following tour is a suggestion only of a route through the garden. A dog-walking route follows the outer boundary of the garden and is clearly marked

still surviving and perhaps unique, record daily rainfall for some 40 years. An album of photographs, showing the building progress of the house between 1924 and 1926 and the garden's development from 1927 to 1936, also exists as an excellent record and resource.

Change of management

Rowland Smith also kept a plant book in which he recorded acquisition and planting details, following the same bed order as the D'Oyly Cartes' planting book. However much essential work, such as thinning the shelterbelts, was never carried out and in the 1970s the lower garden was grazed by Jacob sheep.

When the National Trust acquired the estate in 1982 the garden was badly overgrown and work at first concentrated on creating access paths, fencing, re-instating hedges, modernising cottages and creating a new car park. The first tenants of the garden, Richard and Jane Taylor, began the major task of clearing and replanting and started a programme of reducing and thinning, including the felling of several over-mature trees.

The Courtyard
Seemly Terrace

The Courtyard

From the Courtyard, many of whose climbers and wall plants survive from the D'Oyly Cartes' time, the garden is entered at its westernmost point. Kent's Bed is planted for spring and autumn interest. The planting includes a tiered mix of bulbs, shrubs and small trees, including a myrtle framing the view. Lower Kent's Bed, a small bed against the Saloon window, is full of semi-tender climbers, with a mixture of unusual plants such as eucomia, watsonia, *Grevilla abutilon* and a trumpet vine (*Campsis radicans*), which originates from South America.

Seemly Terrace

Seemly Terrace, backed by a tall beech hedge, screens the former hard tennis court built in the 1920s by Stuarts Granolithic Co., London, and today is used as the garden service area. The terrace consists of a wide stone-paved path with beds either side, created around 1926 to Oswald Milne's design. These beds are planted for spring effect with groups of Japanese cherries (*Prunus shogetsu*) underplanted with double narcissus, dicentra, tulips, camassia, alliums and clumps of *Iris sibirica*.

Seemly Hut, previously used to store tennis equipment, contains a display of information boards relating to the garden. Written into the concrete of its floor is the date 1928, probably the year the tennis court was completed.

The Rill Garden
The Ironwood Tree and West Bank

The Rill Garden

The Rill Garden was designed by Oswald Milne, although the actual design drawings were entrusted to his assistant, John Brandon Jones. With its pools and canalised stream, it was originally planted mostly with roses. However these did not thrive in the humid maritime climate. Today the central island beds are predominantly planted with a mixture of hardy herbaceous and semi-tender perennials of soft pastel shades, such as delphiniums, geraniums, salvia, penstemons, argyranthemum and asters, to create an effect reminiscent of Lady Dorothy's own planting.

At the top of the garden is a wisteria, originally planted in the 1920s, and in the top right corner is an *Itea illcifolia* from China. In the borders adjacent to the walls is a collection of unusual climbers and shrubs, taking advantage of the extra protection offered. They include the twining climber *Dregea sinensis* from China and a *Buddleja lindleyana* from Japan. On the outside wall are several groups of fragrant hedychiums (ginger lilies), a *Rhaphiolepis umbellata* and several cestrums.

The Ironwood Tree and West Bank

At the bottom of the Rill Garden the water cascades towards the Upper and Lower Ponds. Passing the round stone pillars to the Parrotia Lawn, the huge Persian Ironwood Tree (*Parrotia persica*) is on your left. Follow one of the paths up the West Bank for excellent views across the valley. This is a rare area of unimproved grassland, and of particular note are the large anthills, undisturbed for hundreds of years. During the spring and summer months the West Bank is covered with wild flowers and fine grasses, attracting a wide variety of insects and butterflies.

Retrace your steps back to the Rill Garden to explore the house terraces

Left **The Rill Garden**

Right **The West Bank**

The terraces

The relationship between house and garden is intimate at Coleton Fishacre, linked by style and design and through views from the house of the three terraces. Around the house the garden has a firm architectural framework, with walls and terraces which reflect the lines of the house.

These areas are used to shelter tender, mainly sun-loving plants, such as the sub-tropical and powerfully banana-scented michelia. There is also *Camellia sasanqua*, which produces its fragrant deep pink flowers in autumn. The erect and showy spikes of watsonia (the bugle lily), native to South Africa, compete for height with dierama (angels' fishing rods). The originally antipodean leptospermum and New Zealand tea trees add hot shades of crimson and pink.

The house walls shelter a number of fine climbers and wall shrubs, including sweetly perfumed wintersweet, abutilon, *Jasminum mesnyi* and *Pandorea jasminoides*.

The top terrace is one of the most important areas of the garden, accessed directly from the Saloon and the Loggia. The concave pool of the middle terrace is fed by a stream that runs behind the house. Its rounded outline sets off a sculpted otter, designed by local artist Bridget McCrum in 1991 and carved from Cornish Polyphant. The design is based on the original Portland stone sculpture, 'Tarka', by Hugh Pallister, removed in 1982.

The lower terrace, or Hot Border, is divided by a larger rectangular pool, in which grows the water hawthorn, with fragrant black-antlered white flowers in spring. Amongst the planting scheme are *Salvia confertiflora* from Brazil, *Canna* 'Wyoming' and *Canna indica*, alstroemeria, crocosmia and *Lobelia tupa*. The *Crinodendron hookerianum* (Chilean lantern tree) was planted by the D'Oyly Cartes in 1926. The drystone walls perfectly complement the hot colours and enhance the self-seeded Mexican daisies, *Erigeron karvinskianus*.

Left The walls of the lower terrace pool have been colonised by Mexican daisies, *Erigeron karvinskianus*

Far left (above) The 'hot' colours of *Lobelia tupa* in the lower terrace

Far left (below) Dahlia 'Moonfire' in front of the house

Opposite Slate steps down to the terraces

The Tulip Tree

Below the terraces and fed by the cascade of the Rill Garden are the Upper and Lower Ponds in a naturalistic setting, where water-loving plants cluster at the stream's edge. But looking up, you'll see a tree marking a spot special to the D'Oyly Cartes.

Rising out of the lawn below the terraces, like a ship's mast against the backdrop of the sea, stands the Tulip Tree. This tree, *Liriodendron tulipifera*, is resplendent in early summer with green-yellow and orange flowers. One of the first trees planted in the garden in 1926, by 1986 the Tulip Tree had attained 1.24 metres in girth, with a lovely 'candelabra' shape given by its three trunks, possibly a result of being pollarded.

The tree was clearly significant to the D'Oyly Cartes: Patch, their Dalmatian, who can be seen sitting with Rupert on the map painting in the Library (see page 26), is buried beneath it. The tree is underplanted with groups of small bulbs for spring effect and forms the centrepiece of a large open-lawned glade, framed by planting including pittosporum and bounded by the stream.

Above The Tulip Tree only flowers in June and July

Left The stream pools a second time in the Lower Pond, created by damming in 1926; the gigantic rhubarb-like gunnera are a prominent feature

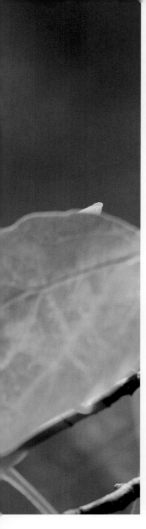

Right The Quarry that supplied the stone to build the house, colonised by agapanthus; the Gazebo is above

The Tree
of Heaven
The Quarry

The Tree of Heaven

Another significant tree in the Coleton Fishacre collection is the towering Tree of Heaven (*Ailanthus altissima*). It is at its most decorative in late summer, when its bunches of red seeds are set off by the handsome frond-like leaves. It comes from China, where it is used in traditional medicine.

The Quarry

The Quarry provided much of the stone to build the house, enabling it literally to come from the ground on which it was built. A temporary railway was built to transport the stone to the site of the house (see page 7). The only plants noted as introduced by the D'Oyly Cartes here were fig trees. Today, plants have been added, such as agapanthus, puya, furcraea and olearia, to tie in with the silver-grey rock face and scree and to take advantage of the convected heat produced by the stone. There is still a fig tree lower down and, higher up, *Erica arborea* has self-seeded.

The path leading from the Quarry passes through a wooded area where, amongst others, a snowdrop tree, two handkerchief trees and several flowering dogwoods grow. A wisteria winds itself up into the canopy of the trees above. Dotted throughout this area are some of the plantsman Roy Lancaster's Tasmanian collection of *Leptospermum lanigerum*.

The Glade
Newfoundland
and Bluebell Wood

The Glade

From the Tree of Heaven there is a tantalising glimpse of the sea. Leading down to the Glade, the planting includes a group of liquidamber, magnolia, hydrangea and a champion specimen of *Cornus capitata*. This area is one of lush and exotic planting. In the lower half of the Glade grow several interesting trees, including *Podocarpus totara*, *Agathis australis*, pseudopanax and *Sciadopitys verticillata*, also known as the Japanese umbrella pine.

Newfoundland and Bluebell Wood

Take the right-hand path to the dramatic rocky outcrop known as Newfoundland, a large area at the extreme south of the garden under a canopy of old beech and pine. Originally called Newfoundland Meadow, the area is predominantly holm oak and conifer woodland. Climbing up the rocky path and steps, which add to the wild, natural character of the area and give good views of the stream, you reach Bluebell Wood. This area of mixed birch and chestnut, with occasional sorbus and carpeted with bluebells in the spring, phases into the adjoining shelterbelts, screened with olearia and berberis at the western edge. Beyond lies an area of now 'lost' garden known as the Hanging Valley; the original D'Oyly Carte garden extended out to the south-west of the existing and ran down to the coast.

Tree Fern Glade
Long Close and Cathedral Bank

Tree Fern Glade

Retrace your steps back down the hill, making your way carefully down the steeply descending stepped path, through the Tree Fern Glade in the lower garden. This area, almost like a dell, a valley within a valley, has its own character, with a rustic chestnut bridge, hydrangea and New Zealand tree ferns.

Access through a wooden gate leads you onto the coastal footpath and to a viewing point at the head of Pudcombe Cove (see page 44), from where the massed tiers of planting and steepness of the valley are very apparent.

Long Close and Cathedral Bank

Past the shelterbelt the path emerges above a wide slope to reveal another fine sea view. The Long Close, leading steeply uphill away from the coast to the east, opens up into a spectacular large open glade known as Cathedral Bank – a tall, steep hillside with remnants of unimproved grassland rising to the north. Just before climbing the steps there are banks of camellia and a trio of lily of the valley trees from Madeira (*Clethra arborea*). Half-way up the Cathedral Bank there are spectacular views of the coast from the summerhouse erected in 2009.

Pudcombe Cove

At the top of Cathedral Bank, take the path to the right leading to a clearing, known as Scout's Point. On a clear day the lighthouse at Start Point can be seen and, closer to home, the Day Mark. Below, at the bottom of the cliffs, is Pudcombe Cove.

Here, the D'Oyly Cartes created a reinforced concrete tidal bathing pool and jetty, built between 1929 and 1931. The cove was accessed by steep concrete steps that zigzagged down the cliff. From the sea the cove could be reached by the jetty, built from shingle from the beach and running out 60 metres or so into the sea. Considerable investment and effort were made to provide comfort and convenience for the family and guests. Facilities included a changing hut decoratively faced with pebbles, a sun-bathing platform and a cold-water shower, made by diverting a stream. The bathing pool is roughly oval in shape and located on the south-east side of the cove to ensure maximum sun.

The cove has been inaccessible to visitors since 2001, due to the perilous state of the steps caused by coastal erosion and rock falls. The National Trust, in line with its policy not to interfere with natural coastal processes, is allowing nature to take its course, which will mean the eventual loss of the buildings. A detailed survey was undertaken in 2006 to ensure that this information would not be lost.

Top Sailboats in Pudcombe Cove

Above Bathers in Pudcombe Cove

Paddock Wood

Here the garden continues to draw you into its wilder, wooded areas, where nature has been more or less left to take its course. It is a quiet corner of the garden in which to lose yourself and savour some of the sights and sounds of local flora and fauna.

The path takes you through an area known as Paddock Wood, an important and special place given the lack of agricultural 'improvements'. For example, fertilisers haven't been used here since the 1920s, when it was part of the farm at Coleton Barton. Left to its own devices, the biodiversity of Paddock Wood has improved, leading to conditions much closer to nature, where native and wild species abound.

Before motorisation and tractors, the gardeners at Coleton Fishacre used a pony and trap. In those days this area was a grass paddock where the horses used around the garden were kept – hence the name Paddock Wood.

The path was re-opened by the National Trust in 1998 and the area planted up as additional shelterbelt. As the trees grow, selective thinning of the conifers and broadleaves will be carried out, opening views and encouraging open mixed woodland with grass, managed for wildlife. From here there are fine views of the sea and the Mew Stone, a rocky island to the west.

Above The mixed and 'unimproved' nature of Paddock Wood make it a rich and diverse habitat

Right Head Gardener Jack Sharland working with pony and trap

The Gazebo

Above **The Gazebo**

At the Gazebo the lower garden is laid out before you. Below it is the Quarry, where stone for the house was taken, and from the Gazebo a view of the sea and the Blackstone Rocks is framed by pines.

The hexagonal Gazebo, with its stone pillars and wooden superstructure and planted with climbers including wisteria, was designed by Oswald Milne in 1926. Originally there would have been a clear view back to the house but this is now screened by a large cryptomeria.

There would also have been a similar view, to the sea from the Gazebo, from the house when it was first built. The D'Oyly Cartes planned it this way and planted trees so that the finest views would be happened upon, adding to their effect. From the Gazebo the eye-catching tree to your right is the Tree of Heaven (see page 41).

The path from the Gazebo, with its dry, south-facing banks on either side, is one of the mildest areas of the garden and is planted with exotics including yucca, bromelia, protea and echium.

The Bowling Green Lawn

The Bowling Green Lawn with the south-facing Wellington's Wall affords glorious sea views, and its wonderfully open aspect makes it a prime spot both for picnickers and for the plants that thrive here in the sun, sea and salt air.

The Bowling Green Lawn leads back to the top terrace via a paved circle set in the lawn, its centre formed by stacked terracotta flower pots, another Arts and Crafts touch. The lawn is bound to the north by Wellington's Wall, built in 1936 according to a note in Rowland Smith's plant book. Its raised bed, largely replanted in 1997, is south-facing and harbours sun-loving plants such as *Cistus romneya* (with its flower the appearance of a large fried egg), rosemary and gaura. The dense screen of myrtle, escallonia and cornus encloses the lawn and this, together with the planting which leads up to the full height of the pine shelterbelt to the north, gives the area a feeling of quiet seclusion.

From the lawn near the house you can see, to the north, the ship's bell, used to call the family and any guests back from Pudcombe Cove at the end of the day.

As you walk back past the house to the car park (which was originally a fruit orchard supporting geese, chickens and bees) you can see a large white building. This is the Motor Lodge, which housed the family's cars and part of which was used for stabling horses. It also included accommodation for two gardeners and the chauffeur. Despite its rural setting, Coleton Fishacre was largely self-sufficient. As well as electricity being supplied by a diesel generator in the Motor Lodge, it had its own water supply, sewage system and even a private petrol pump.

Above The Bowling Green Lawn

Left *Cistus romneya*

Still more to explore

The wider landscape, surrounded by farmland, gives the context and reason for the building of Coleton Fishacre on this site. Originally an area of farmland with orchards, some woodland and a stream, it remained largely unchanged until the D'Oyly Cartes purchased the 962-acre estate and began to build the house and create the garden.

The area between Pudcombe Cove and Froward Point to the south-west is a designated Site of Special Scientific Interest, due to its variety of flora and fauna, including the nationally rare toadflax-leaved St John's wort. The cliff ground to the north-east is an area of unimproved grassland, and the gardens above are being managed to create corridors to link up to the coast for the benefit of species such as bats, swallows and butterflies.

As well as the natural landscape of the estate, there are a number of interesting buildings, which give some clues to the history of the wider estate. These, which include the Second World War installation at Brownstone Battery (the military fortification at Froward Point) and Coleton Camp, are well worth exploring. Holiday cottages on the estate range from the large Higher Brownstone Farmhouse and the Chauffeur's Flat to simpler farm cottages, and are a wonderful base from which to explore. See the inside back cover for booking details. Enjoy your visit and we look forward to welcoming you back!

Above and left Take time to explore, pause and indulge in nature